MOSHI MOSHI

A TRAVELOGUE

A COLORFUL
JOURNEY OF
JAPAN THROUGH
CULTURE, FOOD,
FASHION, AND
MORE

WINNIE LIU

ULYSSES
PRESS

PUBLISHED BY:
ULYSSES PRESS
PO BOX 3440
BERKELEY, CA 94703
WWW.ULYSSESPRESS.COM

ISBN: 978-1-64604-551-8

PRINTED IN COLOMBIA
10 9 8 7 6 5 4 3 2 1

ACQUISITIONS EDITOR: CASIE VOGEL
MANAGING EDITOR: CLAIRE CHUN
PROJECT EDITOR: SHELONA BELFON
EDITOR: RENEE RUTLEDGE
PROOFREADER: BERET OLSEN
ILLUSTRATIONS: WINNIE LIU

CHAPTER 1

Fantasy

AUGUST 24– OCTOBER 20

JAPAN HAD ALWAYS SEEMED FANTASTICAL TO ME, BUT I ADMIT A LOT OF THAT PERCEPTION CAME FROM THE MEDIA I CONSUMED. WHAT WOULD IT BE LIKE TO SET FOOT FOR REAL IN THIS COUNTRY AND STAY FOR MONTHS? I FOUND OUT WHEN I ARRIVED IN TOKYO IN THE FALL OF 2018.

Hi there, I'm **Winnie**

よろしく

I'M AN ILLUSTRATOR AND DESIGNER WORKING AND LIVING IN BROOKLYN, NEW YORK, BUT I HAIL ORIGINALLY FROM THE RAINY PARADISE OF VANCOUVER. I'M A PASSIONATE FOODIE, HUNTER OF UNDER-THE-RADAR SPOTS, AND PINK FANATIC.

IN THE FALL OF 2018, I RECEIVED THE CHANCE TO STUDY IN TOKYO AS AN EXCHANGE STUDENT AT MUSASHINO ART UNIVERSITY. I HAD GROWN UP OBSESSING OVER JAPANESE ANIME AND MANGA, CUISINE, "KAWAII" (CUTE) CULTURE, AND FASHION. I WAS PURSUING A CREATIVE CAREER BECAUSE I WAS INSPIRED BY THE WORK OF MANY JAPANESE MANGA ARTISTS AND ILLUSTRATORS, SO NEEDLESS TO SAY, THIS TRIP WAS— WARNING: LAMEST CLICHÉ EVER—TRULY A

Dream Come True.

COME ALONG FOR THIS (UN-) BIASED DIARY OF MY WONDERFUL TIME IN JAPAN! I HOPE MY JOURNEY CAN TRANSPORT YOU THERE AND ALSO SERVE AS A GUIDE IF YOU EVER TRAVEL TO THE LAND OF THE RISING SUN.

EXPLORING

TOKYO
東京

WITH TURTLE FATHER
(MY DAD'S NICKNAME)

I DRAGGED POPS AROUND FOR A FEW DAYS TO SIGHTSEE BEFORE MY SEMESTER BEGAN.

BASASHI (HORSE SASHIMI) MIGHT SOUND CRAZY, BUT I HAD TO TRY IT! THE MEAT HAD A SURPRISINGLY NICE SPICY AFTERTASTE.

OMOIDE YOKOCHŌ
思い出横丁

FOR YAKITORI SKEWERS

IZAKAYA FARE

OMOIDE YOKOCHŌ IS A CHARMING BACK ALLEY MAZE FULL OF IZAKAYAS (JAPANESE BARS). WALKING THROUGH HERE IS FUN, BUT THE FOOD IS UNDERWHELMING AS IT CATERS MORE TO THE HORDES OF TOURISTS THAN TO LOCALS. FIVE OF THE SHOPS IN THIS TINY 650-FOOT ALLEY ARE OWNED BY THE SAME PERSON AND SERVE THE SAME FOOD. MY SUGGESTION: GO FOR THE EXPERIENCE, BUT EAT DINNER ELSEWHERE!

SHINJUKU
新宿

ALL OF THE BRIGHT LIGHTS, FLASHING LED COMMERCIALS, AND ENDLESS SKYSCRAPERS REALLY MAKE SHINJUKU THE EPITOME OF A FUTURISTIC TOKYO. AT THE SAME TIME, JAPAN REALLY BALANCES THE CHAOS AND THE CALM. YOU MIGHT FIND A SERENE SHRINE JUST AROUND THE CORNER FROM NEON OVERLOAD.

AND FINALLY . . .

1.5 HOURS TO TOKYO
(UNFORTUNATELY)

Tachikawa

MY DORM WAS IN TACHIKAWA, A CITY IN THE WESTERN TOKYO METROPOLIS. THE SUBURBAN FEELING OFFERED A NICE CONTRAST TO BUSY TOKYO.

WHY IS JAPAN SO KAWAII?

OF COURSE THIS IS THE CITY MASCOT.

UHH . . .
ETO . . .
ANO . . .

zaru udon

(CHILLED UDON WITH DIPPING SAUCE)

I DIDN'T KNOW UDON COULD BE SO TASTY BEFORE I WENT TO JAPAN. THERE WAS A DELICIOUS FAST-SERVICE UDON CHAIN NAMED MARUGAME SEIMEN NEARBY. I CLAMPED UP AND FORGOT ALL OF MY JAPANESE THE FIRST TIME THAT I VISITED, AWKWARDLY LEAVING MY WHITE DAD TO ORDER FOR ME. I'VE SINCE MASTERED THE MENU!

SUBURBAN SIGN #1

Mama Chari

SHORT FOR MAMA CHARIOTS, THESE ELECTRICALLY POWERED BIKES OFTEN FEATURE SEATS AND GENEROUS BASKETS. BUSY MOTHERS CAN BE SEEN HAULING GROCERIES AND FERRYING CHILDREN AROUND THE NEIGHBORHOOD ON THEM.

EVERYONE SEEMS TO OWN ONE.

DACHSHUND OBSESSION

RIDICULOUSLY CUTE SCHOOLKIDS

COMMUNIST GYOZA

I WENT TO A FAMOUS GYOZA SHOP NEAR TACHIKAWA STATION. THE DUMPLINGS THERE ARE THE SIZE OF A CLOSED FIST. THE PLACE IS NICKNAMED "COMMUNIST GYOZA" FOR ITS STRICT RULES ABOUT ORDERING—YOU HAVE TO ORDER AT LEAST 1 PLATE OF GYOZA AND A DRINK. YOU MAY ONLY ORDER ONCE. NO TAKEOUT.

ARIGATOU GOZAIMASU

JAPANESE AMBULANCES

ARE SO polite & respectful

THEY ANNOUNCE THEIR PRESENCE WITH COURTEOUS VOICE-OVER.

I WANTED TO PINCH HIS CHEEKS SO BADLY!

ADVENTURES AT THE

スーパー

"SŪPĀ"
(SUPERMARKET)

Supermarket Anthems

USUALLY SOUND LIKE OVERLY ENTHUSIASTIC ELEVATOR MUSIC . . . I'VE HEARD SONGS ABOUT FISH AND SWEET POTATOES!

THE MOST EXPENSIVE GRAPES EVER SOLD IN JAPAN WENT FOR:

1,100,000 ¥!

($8,286 USD)

Perfect Produce

JAPANESE PRODUCE, ESPECIALLY FRUIT, MIGHT BE SOME OF THE MOST DELICIOUS BUT EXPENSIVE IN THE WORLD. IN FACT, IT'S COMMON TO GIVE SUPER-FANCY FRUITS AS A PRESENT.

EVERY EVENING AROUND 7 PM AT MY LOCAL **maruetsu** SUPERMARKET, THE PREPARED FOODS WERE HEAVILY DISCOUNTED.

WAITING WITH OTHER CUSTOMERS FOR THE WORKERS TO SLAP ON THE DAILY DISCOUNT STICKERS MADE ME FEEL LIKE A LOCAL.

TAKE-OUT TREASURES

ANOTHER UNIQUE ASPECT IS THE SECTION DEDICATED TO TAKEOUT DISHES. COMMON OPTIONS INCLUDE ODEN (FISHCAKE, EGGS, DAIKON, ETC., STEWED IN A DASHI BROTH), STIR-FRIES, PICKLES, AND MORE. THERE ARE ALSO SELF-SERVE FRIED FOODS AND YAKITORI THAT YOU BOX UP YOURSELF.

20% OFF OR MORE!

*PERCHING LIKE A HAWK IS OPTIONAL.

UNIQUE INGREDIENTS

THERE ARE ENTIRE TOFU SECTIONS AT THE SUPERMARKET!

NATTO IS A FERMENTED SOYBEAN PRODUCT WITH A STICKY, SLIMY TEXTURE. IT IS AN ACQUIRED TASTE AS IT'S QUITE BITTER, BUT HIGH-QUALITY ONES ARE ACTUALLY VERY DELICIOUS.

JAPANESE MAYO IS SLAPPED ON COUNTLESS DISHES. IT'S EGGIER AND TANGIER THAN ITS AMERICAN COUNTERPART—A REAL TREAT.

MOCHI ARE CHEWY RICE CAKES FOUND IN A VARIETY OF SAVORY AND SWEET DISHES.

SASHIMI IS AVAILABLE IN SO MANY MORE OPTIONS IN JAPAN, AND IT'S CHEAPER.

AMBERJACK IS SO GOOD!

MENTAIKO, A SPICY COD ROE, MAKES FOR A DELICIOUS TOPPING ON SPAGHETTI. IT'S A PERFECT INSTANT FUSION MEAL.

SOY SAUCE IN COUNTLESS VARIETIES

MISO (COMES IN INSTANT PACKS TOO)

WASABI

MIRIN IS A SWEET RICE WINE USED OFTEN IN COOKING. IT MAKES FOOD TASTE INHERENTLY JAPANESE TO ME.

KATSUOBUSHI (BONITO OR SKIPJACK TUNA) IS A MAIN INGREDIENT IN MAKING DASHI, A BROTH WITH LOTS OF UMAMI FLAVOR THAT FORMS THE BASE OF MANY JAPANESE SOUPS, SAUCES, AND MORE.

COOKING SAKE

NAKANO

I TRIED THE INFAMOUS 8-FLAVOR SOFT SERVE FROM DAILY CHIKO! IT WAS SURPRISINGLY GOOD, BUT YOU NEED TO EAT IT SUPER FAST.

NAKANO IS A SPECIAL WARD IN TOKYO. THERE'S AN AMAZING SHOPPING ARCADE HERE CALLED NAKANO BROADWAY, WHICH WAS MY FAVORITE PLACE TO BUY ANIME GOODS AND OTHER KNICKKNACKS. I HAVE A PARTICULAR WEAKNESS FOR THE SAILOR MOON MERCHANDISE AND TINY FAKE FOOD PARAPHERNALIA.

CUTE!!

I MET KAILA, THE KAWAII LIFESTYLE BLOGGER BEHIND RAINBOWHOLIC. I'VE LONG ADMIRED HER POSITIVE ENERGY AND ADORABLE CONTENT, SO IT WAS VERY SPECIAL TO SEE HER IN THE FLESH AT LAST!

！FRESH STRAWBERRY

KAWAGOE

NICKNAMED "LITTLE EDO," THIS HISTORIC MERCHANT AND CASTLE TOWN IS TEEMING WITH BEAUTIFUL ARCHITECTURE. TRAVELING TO KAWAGOE MAKES FOR A GREAT DAY TRIP FROM TOKYO—IT'S EASILY ACCESSIBLE AND OFFERS A COMPLETELY DIFFERENT PACE OF LIFE COMPARED TO THE BIG CITY.

TOWN MASCOT

SWEET POTATO CHIPS

SWEET POTATO LUNCH SET

KAWAGOE IS THE TOWN OF SWEET POTATOES, AND IT REALLY SHOWS!

Sweet Potato Soft Serve

HARAJUKU

THIS FASHIONABLE AREA IN TOKYO WILL ALWAYS HAVE A SPECIAL PLACE IN MY HEART FOR ITS KAWAII CULTURE AND STREET FASHION, BOTH MAJOR INTERESTS OF MINE AFTER ART. TO THIS DAY, MY HEART BEATS WITH EXCITEMENT WHEN I COME HERE.

MY *forever* LOVE

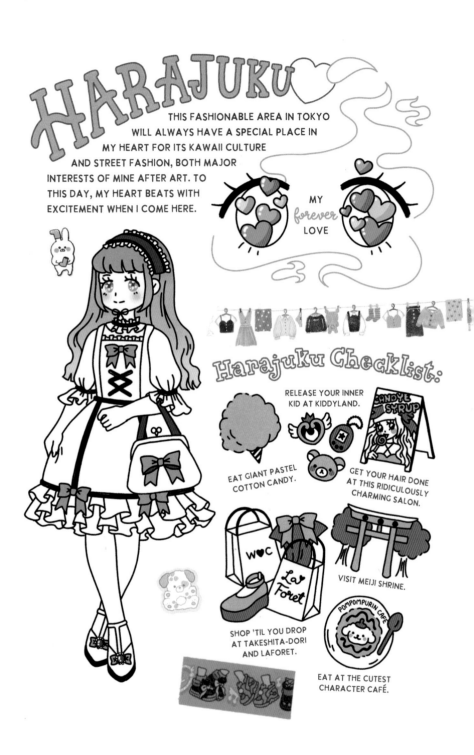

Harajuku Checklist:

RELEASE YOUR INNER KID AT KIDDYLAND.

CANDYE SYRUP

EAT GIANT PASTEL COTTON CANDY.

GET YOUR HAIR DONE AT THIS RIDICULOUSLY CHARMING SALON.

W♥C

La Foret

VISIT MEIJI SHRINE.

POMPOMPURIN CAFE

SHOP 'TIL YOU DROP AT TAKESHITA-DORI AND LAFORET.

EAT AT THE CUTEST CHARACTER CAFÉ.

EVERYTHING & EVERYONE IS SO CUTE,

IT MAKES ME WANT TO CRY.

FAVE SHOPS

WEGO
LiZ LiSA
closetchild
AnkRouge
Angelic Pretty

KAWAII MONSTER Cafe

& SHIBUYA

ONE TRAIN STOP AWAY IS SHIBUYA! THERE'S LOTS TO DO IN THIS AREA, BUT I MUST ADMIT MY VICE IS SHOPPING AT SHIBUYA 109, A CYLINDRICAL MALL DEDICATED TO TRENDY FASHION. I COULD SPEND AN ENTIRE WEEK THERE (AND PROBABLY A MORTGAGE).

HACHIKO

HACHIKO WAS AN AKITA WHO FAITHFULLY AWAITED THE RETURN OF HIS DEAD MASTER AT SHIBUYA STATION EVERY DAY FOR ALMOST 10 YEARS. THIS BITTERSWEET TALE INSPIRED MY DAD TO ADOPT HIS OWN AKITA.

SO MANY

CUTE CLOTHES

my

WALLET DIED...

109

POKÉMON SCREECH

SHOP 'TIL YOU DROP

I CAN'T DECIDE IF THE UNBELIEVABLY SHRILL VOICES OF THE SHOP GIRLS ARE SWEET OR SCARY . . .

Point Cards

AKA EVIDENCE THAT MY SHOPAHOLIC NATURE INTENSIFIES IN JAPAN...

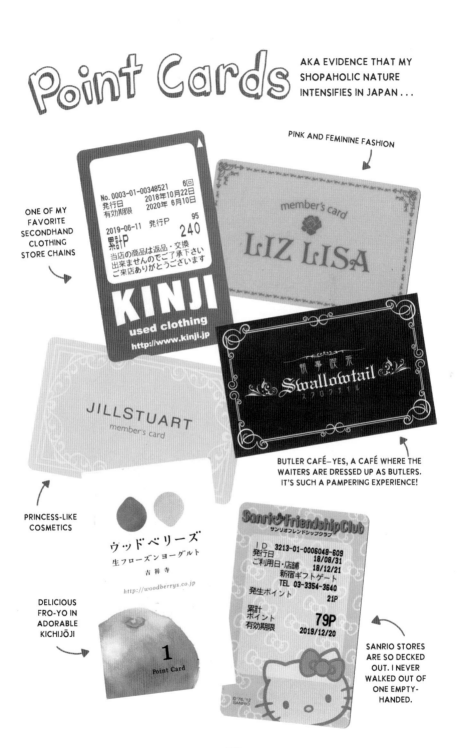

PINK AND FEMININE FASHION

ONE OF MY FAVORITE SECONDHAND CLOTHING STORE CHAINS

No. 0003-01-00348521　6回
発行日　　2018年 10月22日
有効期限　2020年 6月10日

2019-06-11　発行P　95
累計P　　　　　240

当店の商品は返品・交換
出来ませんのでご了承下さい
ご来店ありがとうございます

KINJI
used clothing
http://www.kinji.jp

member's card
LIZ LISA

JILLSTUART
member's card

執事喫茶
Swallowtail
スワロウテイル

BUTLER CAFÉ—YES, A CAFÉ WHERE THE WAITERS ARE DRESSED UP AS BUTLERS. IT'S SUCH A PAMPERING EXPERIENCE!

PRINCESS-LIKE COSMETICS

ウッドベリーズ
生フローズンヨーグルト
吉祥寺

http://woodberrys.co.jp

1
Point Card

DELICIOUS FRO-YO IN ADORABLE KICHIJŌJI

Sanrio Friendship Club
サンリオフレンドシップクラブ

ID　3213-01-0006048-609
発行日　　　　　18/08/31
ご利用日・店舗　18/12/21
　　新宿ギフトゲート
TEL 03-3354-3640
発生ポイント　　　21P
累計
ポイント　　　　79P
有効期限　2019/12/20

©'76,'12
SANRIO

SANRIO STORES ARE SO DECKED OUT. I NEVER WALKED OUT OF ONE EMPTY-HANDED.

KŌENJI

KŌENJI IS A HUB OF UNDERGROUND CULTURE, ALTERNATIVE MUSIC, PUNK ROCK, AND VINTAGE CLOTHING. ONCE THE SUN SETS, GRAB A DRINK FROM ONE OF THE NUMEROUS IZAKAYA BARS AND SEE A LIVE PERFORMANCE AT A LOCAL VENUE.

I EXPLORED THIS AREA WITH A NEW FRIEND FROM SCHOOL NAMED RIHO. OUR SHARED LOVE OF ALTERNATIVE FASHION AND SUBCULTURES BRIDGED A LOT OF THE LANGUAGE BARRIER. WALKING AROUND WITH OUR COLORFUL HAIR SURE MADE US STAND OUT AS A DUO!

RIHO

THIS HOLE-IN-THE-WALL TEMPURA JOINT IS FAMOUS FOR ITS DEEP-FRIED EGGS. THE MENU IS ALL IN HANDWRITTEN JAPANESE, SO DINING HERE CAN FEEL DAUNTING, BUT I PROMISE IT'S WORTH IT.

A COZY CAFÉ SERVING UP "KID'S MEALS," BUT FOR ADULTS!

THIS ADORABLE TREE-HOUSE THEMED CAFÉ IS DECKED OUT WITH NATURE DECORATIONS AND BEAUTIFUL MURALS. ORDERS ARE PLACED BY CALLING THE WAITRESS WITH A PHONE ATTACHED TO THE WALL!

Vending MACHINE

THIRST DOESN'T EXIST IN JAPAN.

THERE'S A BIG BROTHER VERSION THAT FILMS YOU, THEN DISPLAYS ADS BASED ON YOUR APPEARANCE (AGE, SEX, STYLE, ETC.).

NATION

YOU KNOW HOW THERE ARE MORE SHEEP THAN PEOPLE IN NEW ZEALAND? THAT'S WHAT IT FEELS LIKE IN JAPAN, BUT THE SHEEP ARE VENDING MACHINES. THEY'RE TRULY AT EVERY CORNER AND OFTENTIMES SELL PRODUCTS OTHER THAN DRINKS, SUCH AS UMBRELLAS, MASKS, AND MEALS.

Kichijōji

ONE OF MY FONDEST MEMORIES IN KICHIJŌJI IS MY FIRST DATE WITH MIU. WE WERE PAIRED TOGETHER FOR A SCHOOL PROJECT, WENT TO AN ITALIAN RESTAURANT TO GET TO KNOW EACH OTHER BETTER, AND QUICKLY BECAME BEST PALS.

Cat Cafe

CAPYNEKO CAFÉ: THIS ANIMAL CAFÉ HAS CRIMINALLY CUTE CATS AND ONE SPECIAL CAPYBARA.

靴下屋

Socks!

KUTSUSHITA-YA: I BOUGHT SOCKS WITH A SOCK PATTERN HERE. I'M STILL GIDDY ABOUT IT.

INOKASHIRA PARK FELT LIKE A COUSIN TO BROOKLYN'S PROSPECT PARK, THOUGH IT MAY HAVE BEEN MY HOMESICKNESS TALKING.

KICHIJŌJI IS ONE OF TOKYO'S MOST DESIRABLE NEIGHBORHOODS TO LIVE IN FOR GOOD REASON. IT'S GOT A CHARMING, SLOW-PACED RESIDENTIAL VIBE BUT STILL HAS FUN BACK ALLEYS TO EXPLORE AND EASY PROXIMITY TO THE CITY'S MAJOR TRAIN STATIONS. I WOULD ALSO LIVE HERE IF GIVEN THE CHANCE!

ONE OF THE AREA'S BIGGEST HIGHLIGHTS IS THE:

Ghibli Museum

SATOU

Menchi-katsu

KICHIJŌJI SATOU: THE MENCHI-KATSU (FRIED MEAT PATTIES) HERE ARE DIVINE . . . IT'S WORTH THE QUEUE!

THIS CHARMING INSTITUTION CELEBRATES STUDIO GHIBLI'S FILMS WITH ROTATING EXHIBITIONS, A MAGICAL SHOP, AND A THEMED CAFÉ. DURING MY VISIT, THE SPECIAL FEATURE WAS A GALLERY CELEBRATING THE FOOD IN THE VARIOUS MOVIES. I GET HUNGRY JUST THINKING ABOUT IT!

GHIBLI MUSEUM MITAKA

Dear Diary

MIOTO COULDN'T ATTEND, BUT HER SPIRIT WAS WITH US!

OCTOBER 13

TODAY WAS THE FIRST DAY I FELT A SENSE OF GENUINE COMMUNITY SINCE ARRIVING IN JAPAN. AFTER SCHOOL ENDED, MY CLASSMATES AND I TREKKED TO A GROCERY STORE TO BUY INGREDIENTS FOR A NABE (HOT POT) PARTY. WE WENT OVER TO LULU'S COZY ONE-ROOM APARTMENT, AND ALL 10 OF US HUDDLED AROUND THE TINY TABLE EATING AND LAUGHING TOGETHER. TO BE HONEST, I DON'T EVEN REMEMBER WHAT WE TALKED ABOUT. BUT I DO REMEMBER FEELING WARM AND HAPPY TO BE SURROUNDED BY FRIENDS IN A FOREIGN LAND.

CHAPTER 2

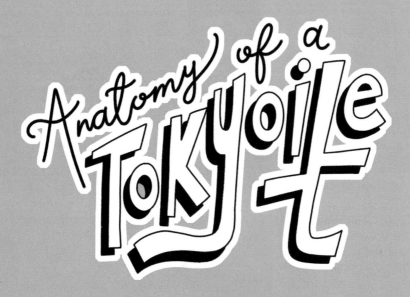

Anatomy of a Tokyoite

IT WAS HARD NOT TO NOTICE A FEW RECURRING CHARACTERS
ONCE I SPENT SOME SUBSTANTIAL TIME IN THIS CITY. ALLOW
ME TO BREAK DOWN SOME COMMON PERSONAS THAT
YOU MIGHT FIND ON THE ROSTER.

Salaryman

EARBUDS TO SHUN THE WORLD

DARK CIRCLES FROM OVERTIME ALL DAY EVERY DAY

DRINK OF CHOICE BECAUSE OF ITS INSTANT ABILITY TO INDUCE DRUNKENNESS

↓

USUALLY HAS ONE READY IN HIS BAG FOR IMMEDIATE EMOTIONAL ERASURE OF THE WORKDAY

POKÉMON GO OR SOME OTHER SILLY APP GAME (OR MAYBE PORN)

WORK DOCUMENTS OR HIDDEN SECRETS?

SAD PREPARED MEAL FROM THE CONBINI

ILL-FITTING SUIT THAT SMELLS OF TOBACCO, IZAKAYA SMOKE, & REGRET

SUBWAY = INSTANT NAP CHAMBER

SCHOOLGIRL

JAPANESE GIRL-NEXT-DOOR BOB HAIRCUT

GONG CHA BUBBLE TEA SHE ABSURDLY WAITED 3 HOURS IN LINE FOR

20 LBS OF CUTE CHARACTER KEYCHAINS

OBSESSED WITH THE STICKERS ON THE LINE MESSAGING APP

PROCLAIMS EVERYTHING IS KAWAII

HOMEMADE BENTO OF YOUR DREAMS

WILL EXPOSE LEGS EVEN IN THE MIDDLE OF THE ARCTIC

Basic Cutie

HIGHLY EDITED "PURIKURA" (KAWAII PHOTO BOOTHS)

HANDBAG HELD IN A PARTICULARLY FEMININE WAY

SOCIAL MEDIA > SOCIALIZING

CURLED STRAIGHT BANGS

INTENSE BLUSH RIGHT BELOW THE EYES

INFURIATINGLY PERFECT HAIR!!!

PRETTY DONE-UP NAILS, ALWAYS

WEARS A SKIRT OR DRESS NO MATTER THE SEASON

WILL EXPOSE LEGS EVEN IN THE WINTER

HIGH HEELS

HIPSTER

SMOKER (OF FANCY IMPORTED CIGARETTES)

PIERCINGS AND FACIAL HAIR

DRINKS COFFEE BREWED FROM HIS OWN ROASTED BEANS, WHICH HE GROUND WITH A EUROPEAN UNICORN HORN PESTLE

LISTENS TO THE TYPE OF MUSIC YOU CAN ONLY FIND ON VINYL: CLASSIC ROCK, '80S, JAZZ . . .

WEARS A WHITE T-SHIRT TO SHOW OFF TATTOO SLEEVE

FITTED JEANS, PROBABLY VINTAGE

OCCUPATION: REQUIRES AN APRON

SEXY EXPOSED ANKLES

LOGO BASEBALL CAP

THICK FOREIGN ACCENT; ALSO ONLY KNOWS 3 PHRASES

LOTS OF SELFIES ...MAYBE TOO MANY SELFIES

CAMERA SLUNG IN FRONT AT ALL TIMES

EXTRA SWEATY ARMPITS

UNFLATTERING FANNY PACK

OBLIGATORY DONNING OF A YUKATA AT LEAST ONCE ON HIS TRIP

STRUGGLES WITH CHOPSTICKS

HAIRY LEGS UNFAMILIAR TO THE JAPANESE EYE

WILL GO HOME WITH A SUITCASE FULL OF SNACKS AS SOUVENIRS

TOES OUT

CHAPTER 3

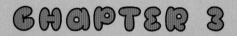

OCTOBER 21–NOVEMBER 3

I HAD 2 WEEKS OFF FROM SCHOOL IN THE AUTUMN, SO I DECIDED
TO EMBARK ON SOME SOLO TRAVELING TO A FEW OF JAPAN'S
OTHER MAJOR CITIES: KYŌTO, ŌSAKA, AND FUKUOKA. PLUS, I WENT
ON AN EXCURSION TO THE FORESTY ART ISLAND OF NAOSHIMA.
COME ALONG FOR THE ADVENTURE!

Kyōto

KYŌTO WAS ONCE THE CAPITAL OF JAPAN, SO IT'S A CITY WITH DEEP-ROOTED CULTURE AND HISTORY.

ONLY ¥700?!

5:00 AM RAMEN

IT WAS FUCKING DELICIOUS.

I'M SORRY FOR DOUBTING YOU...

TOLD YA SO, BITCH.

I DIDN'T SLEEP AT ALL!!!

I TOOK THE OVERNIGHT BUS INSTEAD OF THE SHINKANSEN (BULLET TRAIN) TO SAVE MONEY.

LEARN FROM MY MISTAKE—SACRIFICING YOUR SANITY AND COMFORT ISN'T WORTH THE EXTRA DOLLARS SAVED!

OVERNIGHT DESTRUCTION

I WENT TO HONKE DAIICHI-ASAHI, A POPULAR LOCAL RAMEN SHOP WITH ABSURD OPENING HOURS: 5 AM-2 AM!!! I HAD NOTHING ELSE TO DO AT THE CRACK OF DAWN, SO I THOUGHT I WOULD BEAT THE CROWDS, BUT THERE WAS ALREADY A LONG LINE AT 5 AM... I COULDN'T BELIEVE IT!

AT LEAST I GOT TO EXPLORE FUSHIMI INARI SHRINE BEFORE A TSUNAMI OF TOURISTS ARRIVED.

FUSHIMI INARI

RYOZEN KANNON

KIYOMIZUDERA

So many spiritual awakenings

THE KYŌTO INTERNATIONAL MANGA MUSEUM

HOUSED IN A FORMER ELEMENTARY SCHOOL, THE KYŌTO INTERNATIONAL MANGA MUSEUM IS A MAGNIFICENT CELEBRATION OF MANGA, THE ART OF JAPANESE COMICS. THE INSTITUTE ACTS AS BOTH A MANGA LIBRARY AND HISTORY RESOURCE FOR THE PUBLIC, WITH OVER 300,000 ITEMS AND 50,000 VOLUMES OF MANGA ACCESSIBLE TO VISITORS.

CLICK!

insta-bae

—NOUN, PRONOUNCED INSTA-BA-EH
("BAE" IS A FUNNY COINCIDENCE)
— MEANING: THE ART OF LOOKING FIRE
ON INSTAGRAM

IT WAS A LITTLE HARD TO CAPTURE
THAT "LOCAL FEELING" AMONG
THE HORDES OF TOURISTS.

Kyoto Demographics
(APPROXIMATELY UNTRUE)

70% TOURISTS
25% RESIDENTS
5% CATS

国宝　三十三間堂
SANJŪSANGENDŌ
C 623580
600円

I WON'T SPOIL WHAT'S INSIDE, BUT THIS
PLACE WAS FUCKING NUTS!!! I WAS LEFT
SPEECHLESS. I HIGHLY RECOMMEND VISITING.

LOVELY nosy OBAA-CHAN

I MET A LOVELY GRANDMA RUNNING AN ADORABLE SHOP SELLING HER DAUGHTER'S HANDMADE CERAMICS OF "JIZO" (A BUDDHIST GUARDIAN OF CHILDREN)! SHE BROUGHT OUT SOME RICE CRACKERS AND TEA AND I SAT WITH HER, CHATTING IN JAPANESE FOR WHAT FELT LIKE HOURS. IT AMAZED ME HOW JUST A FEW FEET OUTSIDE, CROWDS OF PEOPLE WERE CRAWLING OVER EACH OTHER, SNAPPING PHOTOS FOR SOCIAL MEDIA AND BUYING MATCHA SOUVENIRS, YET THERE WAS THIS MAGICAL WONDERLAND HIDDEN IN THE CHAOS.

FOOD HIGHLIGHTS

FRIED FISH CAKES
AT NISHIKI MARKET

matcha parfait
AT PATISSERIE GION SAKAI

TONKATSU
(FRIED PORK CUTLET)
AT KATSUKURA SANJO

Fancy Teishoku
(JAPANESE SET MEAL)
AT IZAMA

 **ŌSAKA**

MY HOSTEL WAS CONVENIENTLY LOCATED ONLY 5 MINUTES FROM  **DEN DEN** TOWN (THE ŌSAKA OTAKU HQ). COINCIDENCE OR FATE?

OTAKU

—NOUN, PRONOUNCED OH-TA-KOO

—MEANING: A FAN WITH AN IMMENSE PASSION FOR ANY HOBBY, INTEREST, ETC., THOUGH IT USUALLY REFERS TO A FAN OF ANIME OR MANGA

WELCOME! PLEASE LEAVE YOUR GROSS FANTASIES BEHIND. THIS IS A FAMILY-FRIENDLY ENVIRONMENT.

Den Den Dreams

I THOUGHT THIS MAN WAS SERIOUSLY GOING TO SHIT HIS PANTS AFTER RECEIVING A FLYER FROM A CUTE MAID.

I THINK I'D BE A GREAT CANDIDATE FOR THIS JOB.

LOVE LOVE *MASSAGE*

60 分.........10,000 円

90 分.........12,500 円

120 分........15,000 円

アルバイト

PART-TIME JOB 1,000 円 / HR

MANGA! ANIME! 2D BOYS FALLING IN LOVE AND KISSING UNTIL SUNRISE!

MANDARAKE

(MANDARAKE IS ONE OF JAPAN'S LARGEST USED GOODS RETAIL CHAINS SPECIALIZING IN OTAKU MERCHANDISE.)

SHINSEKAI

THIS AREA IS MODELED AFTER PARIS AND CONEY ISLAND. I WONDER IF THAT EXPLAINS WHY IT FELT TACKY AND SEEDY TO ME—IT WAS THE FIRST TIME I HAD SUCH THOUGHTS ABOUT A PLACE IN JAPAN.

串カツ たこ焼き お好み焼き

COME HERE TO EXPERIENCE . . .

CHEESY RESTAURANTS

GAGGLES OF SALARYMEN

KUSHIKATSU: DEEP-FRIED HEAVEN

DON'T SLEEP ON KUSHIKATSU! EVERYONE SEEMS TO KNOW ABOUT TAKOYAKI AND OKONOMIYAKI, BUT THIS ŌSAKA SPECIALTY OF DEEP-FRIED EVERYTHING ON SKEWERS DIPPED IN A TANGY SOY SAUCE IS SO ♨ HEAVENLY. ✿

DOUBLE DIPPERS, FEEL MY WRATH!*

THIS KUSHIKATSU CHAIN RESTAURANT'S SERVICE BLEW ME AWAY. THE CHEF SHARED HIS RECOMMENDATIONS AND TAUGHT ME HIS FAVORITE WAY TO EAT EACH SKEWER.

*USUALLY SKEWERS ARE DIPPED INTO A COMMUNAL SAUCE POT, BUT SINCE THE COVID-19 PANDEMIC, THE SAUCE IS POURED OVER THE SKEWERS. THIS FLYER'S THREAT IS OUTDATED . . .

ŌSAKANS ARE KNOWN TO BE A LITTLE "ROUGH" AROUND THE EDGES, WHICH IS NOTICEABLE IN THEIR DIALECT AND SPEECH INFLECTIONS. THEY HAVE A REPUTATION AS REBELS AND ARE SUPPOSEDLY THE ONLY JAPANESE PEOPLE WITHOUT AN INFERIORITY COMPLEX TO TOKYO.

THEY WALK ON THE OPPOSITE SIDE COMPARED TO TOKYOITES!

"THE" ŌSAKAN

PANBO

& LONG SOFT CREAM

YEAH, I ATE THEM ALL. DON'T JUDGE.

OF COURSE I TOOK A TOURISTY SELFIE WITH THE GREAT GLICO MAN OF DOTONBORI, ŌSAKA'S ECCENTRIC NIGHTLIFE DISTRICT.

たこぱー
Takoyaki dashi.

FOOD KUIDAORE HEAVEN

LITERALLY MEANS "TO EAT ONESELF TO BANKRUPTCY."

FUCK, THERE GOES MY WAISTLINE.

ŌSAKA'S FOOD SCENE IS INCREDIBLE. MY HIGHLIGHTS INCLUDED:

1. SUSHI AT HARUKOMA HONTEN. THE FOOD AT THIS UNDERSTATED SPOT IN A SHOPPING MARKET WAS SO DELICIOUS THAT I WENT BACK MULTIPLE TIMES!

2. TAKOYAKI IN THE DOTONBORI AREA. I RECOMMEND WALKING FURTHER INTO THE AREA FOR THE EXTRA DELICIOUS JOINTS UNCROWDED BY TOURISTS.

3. STEAK AND COUNTLESS OTHER BEEF CUTS IN THE MINAMISENBA AREA. I CAN'T REMEMBER THE NAME OF THE RESTAURANT, AND I'M SAD ABOUT IT TO THIS DAY.

4. CHEESE TARTS AT PABLO, A CHAIN NATIVE TO ŌSAKA. THE CONFECTIONS ARE TOPPED WITH A TART FRUITY GLAZE THAT CONTRASTS THE CREAMY FILLING NICELY.

5. PHENOMENAL EGG SALAD MADE BY MY HOSTEL HOST. I STILL DREAM ABOUT IT.

6. DOTEYAKI AT IZAKAYA AND KUSHIKATSU RESTARAUNTS. THIS SAVORY MISO STEW OF BEEF TENDONS AND KONJAC WON'T BE WINNING ANY AWARDS FOR MOST ATTRACTIVE DISH, BUT IT'S A DELECTABLE LOCAL SPECIALTY. TRY IT AT AN IZAKAYA OR KUSHIKATSU RESTAURANT.

NAOSHIMA IS A SMALL, SLEEPY ISLAND IN JAPAN'S SETO INLAND SEA, BUT ITS CLAIM TO FAME IS ITS MANY MODERN ART INSTALLATIONS AND MUSEUMS. THE NEIGHBORING ISLANDS OF TESHIMA AND INUJIMA ALSO HOUSE MANY EXHIBITS, AND COLLECTIVELY THE THREE ISLANDS MAKE UP "BENESSSE ART SITE NAOSHIMA." THE JUXTAPOSITION OF A TINY, OFF-THE-GRID TOWN HIDDEN AMONG THE TREES BEING THE HOME OF VERY PRESTIGIOUS MODERN ART PIECES WAS BOTH CONFUSING AND AMUSING.

I RODE A FERRY FROM UNO PORT ON THE MAIN ISLAND OF HONSHU TO ARRIVE AT NAOSHIMA.

I STAYED AT BAMBOO VILLAGE GUESTHOUSE, A HOSTEL NESTLED ATOP A TALL, WOODSY HILL. IT MADE ME FEEL LIKE I WAS IMMERSED IN MOTHER NATURE!

HIGHLIGHTS

CHICHU ART MUSEUM
THE UNIQUE STRUCTURE OF THIS MOSTLY UNDERGROUND MUSEUM PRESERVES THE BEAUTIFUL NATURAL SCENERY AROUND IT.

ART HOUSE PROJECT
THIS EXHIBIT IS COMPRISED OF SEVEN OLD, EMPTY HOUSES TRANSFORMED INTO WORKS OF ART. THE ONE I VISITED FEATURED A REPLICA OF THE STATUE OF LIBERTY.

THE FERRIES ONLY COME AT A FEW SPECIFIC TIMES EACH DAY, SO YOU WILL BE STRANDED IF YOU MISS YOUR BOAT. THIS *DEFINITELY* DIDN'T HAPPEN TO ME.

RICE

DAIKON PICKLE

SOYBEAN AND HIJIKI SALAD

KARAAGE

TAN TAN RAMEN

ONE NIGHT I HAD DINNER AT RAMEN TSUMU, A COZY PLACE THAT SERVED UP IMPRESSIVELY DELICIOUS TAN TAN RAMEN.

BENESSE HOUSE MUSEUM

THIS GRAND MUSEUM AND ADJOINING HOTEL ARE BASED ON THE "COEXISTENCE OF NATURE, ART, AND ARCHITECTURE."

I LOVE YU BATHHOUSE

THIS INSTALLATION CONTRASTS A TRADITIONAL JAPANESE BATHHOUSE STRUCTURE WITH COLORFUL, KITSCHY SCULPTURES, TILES, AND RANDOM OBJECTS. AND YES, YOU CAN BATHE HERE!

FUKUOKA

I SADLY SPRAINED MY FOOT ON MY FIRST DAY HERE, WHICH DRASTICALLY LIMITED MY TRAVEL PLANS . . .

FUKUOKA IS FAMOUS FOR ITS "YATAI," TINY STREET FOOD STALLS THAT LINE THE CANALS. IT'S A GOOD PLACE TO MIX WITH LOCALS AND TOURISTS, BUT I CHICKENED OUT OF DINING AT ONE FROM FEAR THAT MY ELEMENTARY JAPANESE SKILLS WOULD EMBARRASS ME. OH, REGRET! THE YATAI WERE STILL FUN TO SEE FROM THE OUTSIDE, THOUGH.

AT LEAST FUKUOKA HAD SOME DELIGHTFUL CUISINE!

MOTSUNABE

PEAR PARFAIT

HAKATA RAMEN

Mentaiko Spaghetti

THIS SHOP GIRL WAS SO CUTE! WE HAD A LOVELY CONVERSATION IN JAPANESE.

EXPLORING DAIMYO

SO HALLOWEEN WAS SAD: I WAS ALONE WITH A SPRAINED FOOT AND NO COSTUME. TO CHEER MYSELF UP, I VISITED DAIMYO, A TRENDY SHOPPING AREA IN FUKUOKA WITH COOL VINTAGE SHOPS, QUIRKY BARS, AND AN OVERALL UPBEAT VILLAGE VIBE.

THIS HIP OLD LADY OWNED A SICK VINTAGE SHOP. SHE WAS VERY SHOCKED (AND ENCHANTED) BY MY OVERWHELMINGLY PINK ATTIRE.

LOL

A PINK COLONEL SANDERS STATUE STOOD BEFORE HER STOREFRONT!

MANG KING FUNG

営業中

g

G'S BASE
FUKUOKA
SHARE OFFICE FOR GEEKS

FUKUOKA IS KNOWN TO ATTRACT A LOT OF YOUNG PEOPLE WORKING IN START-UPS AND ENTREPRENEURIAL BUSINESSES. THERE'S A FRESH ENERGY TO THE CITY, AND I SPOTTED PLENTY OF SHARED OFFICES SIMILAR TO WEWORK.

NOVEMBER 2

TRAVELING AND SIGHTSEEING BY MYSELF FOR THE PAST WEEK HAS MADE LONELINESS SINK IN EVEN MORE. HOWEVER, STEPPING INTO A STANDING BAR ON A WHIM TONIGHT TURNED MY DAY UPSIDE DOWN. IT WAS AN INTIMATE SPACE THAT HELD NO MORE THAN SIX PEOPLE. AFTER A FEW DRINKS, MY USUAL HESITANCY TO SPEAK JAPANESE QUICKLY VANISHED. I CHATTED MERRILY WITH THE BARTENDER, A YOUNG MARRIED COUPLE, AND A MIDDLE-AGED SALARYMAN, WHO WERE ALL ASTONISHINGLY SWEET. THE SALARYMAN MENTIONED TRAVELING TO CHINA FREQUENTLY FOR BUSINESS, WHICH MADE US REALIZE WE BOTH SPOKE MANDARIN! THEY ALL SEEMED FASCINATED BY EVERYTHING ABOUT ME: MY FIERCELY PINK OUTFIT, MY JAPANESE CONVERSING SKILLS, AND THE COURAGE TO TRAVEL SO MUCH BY MYSELF, HAHA. THOUGH I KNEW WE WOULD NEVER MEET AGAIN, FOR ONE NIGHT IT FELT A LITTLE LIKE FAMILY.

CHAPTER 4

INTERNAL OUTLIER

NOVEMBER 4–DECEMBER 23

THOUGH IT MIGHT BE PREMATURE TO SAY SO, MY TIME IN JAPAN
LED ME TO BELIEVE THAT IT IS EXTREMELY DIFFICULT TO ASSIMILATE
INTO THE CULTURE AS A FOREIGNER (READ: OUTSIDER). I DID FEEL
QUITE ISOLATED OCCASIONALLY, BUT I STARTED TO APPRECIATE
MY UNIQUE PERSPECTIVE AS A VISITOR HERE THE MORE THAT TIME
PASSED. LET'S FINISH OFF MY RECOLLECTION OF THE TRIP WITH
SOME OF MY BIGGEST TAKEAWAYS!

Back to
TOKYO/TACHIKAWA

Super
CUTE
OBAA CHAN

SUBURBAN SIGN #4

KIDS SO CUTE YOUR HEART WILL FEEL LIKE EXPLODING.
DON'T STARE TOO LONG, YOU CREEP!

UNSURE IF I TOLD A CLASSMATE THAT I LIKE DRAWING GIRLS OR THAT I LIKE GIRLS. BOTH ARE TRUE.

Holy Grail
RAMEN

WHO WOULD HAVE THOUGHT THAT THE BEST BOWL
OF TONKOTSU (PORK BROTH) RAMEN I'D EAT IN MY LIFE
WOULD BE AT AN UNASSUMING SPOT IN THE SUBURBS
NEAR SCHOOL . . . LUSCIOUS NOODLES SAT IN A RICH, CREAMY
BROTH TOPPED WITH THICK SLICES OF SUCCULENT PORK BELLY AND FRAGRANT
GROUND SESAME. I WAS FLOORED! I IMAGINE THE AVERAGE TOURIST DOESN'T VISIT
KODAIRA, BUT PLEASE GIVE THE RAMEN AT DORAICHI A TRY IF YOU'RE EVER IN TOWN.

50,000+ VISITORS & 15,000+ ARTISTS!

DESIGN FESTA

NOVEMBER 11

I'M SO HAPPY I WAS ABLE TO ATTEND THE BIGGEST ARTS FESTIVAL IN ASIA! IT WAS AN OVERWHELMINGLY BIG AND BUSY EVENT—I ONLY SAW ABOUT 20 PERCENT OF THE STALLS THERE. STILL, IT WAS SO INSPIRING TO SEE THE MANY TALENTED CREATIVES MAKING A LIVING OFF OF THEIR ART. I HOPE TO EXHIBIT HERE MYSELF SOMEDAY. LIKE USUAL, I SPENT A BIT TOO MUCH MONEY, SO PLEASE ENJOY THIS COLLAGE OF STICKERS I BOUGHT TO JUSTIFY MY PURCHASES.

Cardcaptor Sakura

NOVEMBER 13

I ATTENDED A LIMITED-TIME SPECIAL EXHIBIT FOR CARDCAPTOR SAKURA, ONE OF MY FAVORITE CHILDHOOD ANIMES. THE NOSTALGIA I FELT DURING MY VISIT MADE TEARS FLOW EASILY.

TOO CUTE!

THANKS

©CLAMP · ST/CCSE   NOT FOR SALE

ONE OF THE MAIN EXHIBITS DISPLAYED GIANT BOOKS MODELED AFTER THE CLOW CARD BOOK. THE DESCRIPTIONS EXPLAINED THE HISTORY, CONCEPT, AND MORE OF THE SERIES. I BECAME SO EMOTIONAL.

JAPAN IS STILL waaaaay

OUT IN JAPAN
Love is love

TOO
TOO
TOO

Conservative

THE LGBTQIA+ COMMUNITY STILL FACES MANY LEGAL, SOCIETAL, INTERPERSONAL, AND PROFESSIONAL CHALLENGES IN JAPAN. THERE'S A SERIOUS LACK OF VISIBILITY FOR THEM, SO I WAS GLAD TO SEE POSTERS IN TOKYO AS PART OF A PUBLIC CAMPAIGN TO RAISE AWARENESS ABOUT THE COMMUNITY'S DIVERSITY AND LIFESTYLES.

A FRIEND TOOK ME TO EIYOU, A COZY, INTIMATE CHEF'S TABLE RESTAURANT.

Dining Delight

お酒と料理
えいよう

THE OWNER PREPARED HOME-STYLE DISHES FEATURING A VARIETY OF SEASONAL INGREDIENTS WHILE CHATTING WARMLY WITH HIS PATRONS. WE SAT NEXT TO AN INFURIATINGLY GORGEOUS PAIR OF COWORKERS WHO KEPT DENYING TWO THINGS: THEIR STATUS AS A COUPLE AND THEIR ENGLISH FLUENCY (THEY BOTH SPOKE IT FLAWLESSLY). I WITNESSED A TRULY NEW LEVEL OF JAPANESE HUMBLENESS.

TOKYO 東京

I TRIED TO GO EXPLORE TOKYO AS OFTEN AS I COULD. IT'S AN ENDLESS SPRAWL OF THE OLD AND NEW, THE CALM AND CRAZY. I DON'T THINK I COULD SEE ALL THAT THE CITY HAS TO OFFER—EVEN WITH THREE LIFETIMES.

中央線
CHUO-SEN
SUPREMACY

CHUO-SEN, THE EXPRESS LINE BETWEEN TACHIKAWA AND TOKYO, WAS MY BFF.

Subway STAND-OUTS

IT WAS AN IPHONE. JUST . . . WHY?

JIMIN

THIS DUDE LOOKED OLDER THAN 70, BUT I'M PRETTY SURE HE'S THE LEAD IN A ROCK BAND.

K-POP BANDS LIKE BTS HAVE REALLY BEEN MAKING THEIR MARK IN JAPAN. I MAY HAVE SPOTTED ONE OF THEIR BIGGEST FANS—A 50-SOMETHING-YEAR-OLD GRANDMA DECKED OUT IN FAN MERCHANDISE.

PUBLIC TRANSPORTATION 101

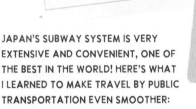

JAPAN'S SUBWAY SYSTEM IS VERY EXTENSIVE AND CONVENIENT, ONE OF THE BEST IN THE WORLD! HERE'S WHAT I LEARNED TO MAKE TRAVEL BY PUBLIC TRANSPORTATION EVEN SMOOTHER:

SUICA AND PASMO CARDS: THESE CONTACTLESS CARDS USED FOR RIDING TRAINS AND BUSES ALSO DOUBLE UP AS A COMMON PAYMENT METHOD AT VENDING MACHINES AND CONVENIENCE STORES. THEY CAN BE PURCHASED AT VENDING MACHINES IN SUBWAY STATIONS AND LOADED UP WITH ANY AMOUNT OF YEN.

SUBWAY LINES: JAPANESE SUBWAY LINES ARE LARGELY MADE UP OF NETWORKS OF VARIOUS PRIVATIZED RAILWAY COMPANIES. AS SUCH, TRANSFERRING TO OTHER LINES FROM THE SAME COMPANY WILL KEEP THE FARES LOWER, WHEREAS CHANGING TO OTHER LINES FROM A DIFFERENT COMPANY WILL INCREASE THE TRAVEL EXPENSE.

JAPAN RAIL PASS (JR PASS): THIS COST-EFFECTIVE AND HANDY TRAVEL OPTION IS AVAILABLE ONLY TO FOREIGN TOURISTS. IT IS VALID FOR ALMOST ALL MAJOR FORMS OF TRANSPORTATION PROVIDED BY THE JR GROUP IN JAPAN, INCLUDING BULLET TRAINS.

AKIHABARA

AKIHABARA IS ONE OF TOKYO'S MOST INTERNATIONALLY FAMOUS NEIGHBORHOODS. CONSIDERED BY MANY TO BE THE EPICENTER OF MODERN JAPANESE OTAKU CULTURE, IT IS THE PLACE TO GO SHOPPING FOR VIDEO GAMES, ANIME, MANGA, COSPLAY SUPPLIES, AND ELECTRONICS. THE AREA FEELS LIKE A TOKYO FEVER DREAM: IT'S DENSELY BUILT-UP, BUT HAS UNIQUE TOUCHES LIKE BLOCKY BUILDINGS IN BOLD PRIMARY COLORS, BLARING VIDEO ADVERTISEMENTS FOR IDOLS, AND MAID CAFÉS ON EVERY CORNER.

RIP

SEGA

SEGA

TO THE ICONIC SEGA BUILDING

figures

BONANZA

Marvelous

Maids

I'VE NEVER VISITED A MAID CAFÉ AS I THOUGHT THE CONCEPT TOO TACKY, BUT THE IDEA OF A CUTE GIRL DRAWING KETCHUP HEARTS ON MY OMURICE IS CHANGING MY OPINION.

Love

48

Gacha Galore

GACHAPON ARE CAPSULE TOY-DISPENSING VENDING MACHINES THAT MANY JAPANESE PEOPLE ARE OBSESSED WITH. THE VARIETY OF PRIZES, FROM GEEKY KEYCHAINS TO MINIATURE FOODS TO HATS FOR YOUR PET, MAKES THE BLIND-BOX EXPERIENCE REALLY FUN (AND SLIGHTLY STRESSFUL)!

CONBINI
Culture

JAPANESE CONVENIENCE STORES (AKA CONBINIS) ARE ACTUALLY CONVENIENT, UNLIKE THE ONES I KNOW IN CANADA AND AMERICA, WHICH MOSTLY JUST SERVE DUBIOUS JUNK FOOD.

THINGS YOU CAN DO AT A CONBINI

 BUY A DELICIOUS AND HEALTHY MEAL FOR DIRT-CHEAP PRICES.

 DRAW MONEY FROM AN ATM AND PAY YOUR BILLS.

USE A FREE TOILET THAT DOESN'T SMELL LIKE A DUMPSTER SITE.

BUY TICKETS TO CONCERTS, MUSEUMS, AMUSEMENT PARKS, THEATERS, AND MORE.

ADULT MAGAZINES ARE VERY ACCESSIBLE IN JAPAN, ESPECIALLY AT CONBINIS, WHERE THEY SIMPLY SIT ON THE SHELF NEXT TO THE OTHER BOOKS. THIS CAN BE A JARRING SIGHT FOR SURE AND IN CONTRAST WITH WHAT I OBSERVE TO BE AN EXTREMELY CLOSED-OFF CULTURE CONCERNING THE DISCUSSION OF SEXUALITY.

RANKING
BASED ON MY TOTALLY BIASED, UNSCIENTIFIC RESEARCH

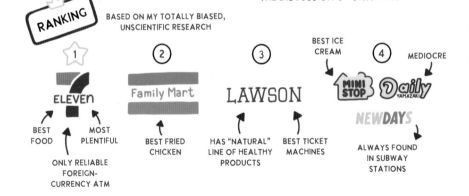

1 7-ELEVEN
BEST FOOD — MOST PLENTIFUL — ONLY RELIABLE FOREIGN-CURRENCY ATM

2 Family Mart
BEST FRIED CHICKEN

3 LAWSON
HAS "NATURAL" LINE OF HEALTHY PRODUCTS — BEST TICKET MACHINES

BEST ICE CREAM
4 MINI STOP — Daily YAMAZAKI — MEDIOCRE
NEWDAYS
ALWAYS FOUND IN SUBWAY STATIONS

FAVORITE munchies

LOOK OUT FOR THESE DELECTABLE TREATS
AT YOUR NEAREST CONVENIENCE STORE! IF
SOMETHING EVER CATCHES YOUR EYE, GIVE IT A SHOT BECAUSE
JAPAN IS NOTORIOUS FOR PEDDLING LIMITED-EDITION ITEMS AND FOODS.

IKEBUKURO

SPRAWLING IKEBUKURO IS ONE OF TOKYO'S LARGEST AND BUSIEST NEIGHBORHOODS.

POKÉMON CENTER MEGA TOKYO

sunshine city

THIS IS THE LARGEST POKÉMON GOODS STORE IN THE CITY!

THERE ARE ALWAYS SO MANY ADORABLE LIMITED-EDITION DESIGNS AVAILABLE; IT'S EVERY FAN'S DREAM. THE STORE IS LOCATED IN THE MASSIVE MALL SUNSHINE CITY, ENSURING A TRIP HERE WILL SURELY BE A FULL-DAY EVENT.

closet child

THIS IS A BRANCH LOCATION OF MY FAVORITE SECONDHAND CLOTHING STORE HAS A CURATED SELECTION OF EXTRAVAGANT ALTERNATIVE FASHIONS. YOU CAN FIND STYLES LIKE LOLITA, PUNK, OTOME, AND MORE.

Milky Way

EVERYTHING AT THIS LAID-BACK CAFÉ IS STAR THEMED! IT'S WAY TOO ENDEARING.

THE AREA IS HOME TO COUNTLESS SHOPPING AND ENTERTAINMENT OPTIONS, PARTICULARLY FOR ANIME AND MANGA FANS. MY ONE-DAY ITINERARY IN IKEBUKURO FOCUSED ALMOST EXCLUSIVELY ON SUCH INTERESTS . . .

K-BOOKS

THOUGH THIS CHAIN CAN BE FOUND THROUGHOUT JAPAN SELLING ANIME, MANGA, AND ADJACENT HOBBY GOODS, THE INVENTORIES OF THE MANY LOCATIONS HERE SPECIFICALLY CATER TO WOMEN.

animate × OURAN

Swallowtail

SWALLOWTAIL IS THE WORLD'S FIRST BUTLER CAFÉ, THE MALE EQUIVALENT OF MAID CAFÉS. BUTLER CAFÉS CATER TO FEMALE OTAKU: PATRONS HERE ARE SERVED BY HANDSOME, SUAVE MEN ROLE-PLAYING DOMESTIC SERVANTS ATTENDING TO ARISTOCRACY.

OTAKU SUPERSTORE ANIMATE RUNS ITS OWN COLLABORATION CAFÉ. THE MENU FEATURES REGULARLY CHANGING ITEMS INSPIRED BY VARIOUS ANIME AND MANGA.

I FEEL LIKE A KID IN A BIG CANDY STORE WITH ENDLESS TEMPTATION!

SHIMOKITAZAWA

WHILE IKEBUKURO IS ONE OF MY FAVORITE AREAS IN TOKYO TO SHOP FOR FANDOM ITEMS, SHIMOKITAZAWA IS MY PREFERRED PLACE TO SHOP FOR COOL SECONDHAND FASHION. THIS OFFBEAT DISTRICT EASILY ATTRACTS HIPSTERS WITH ITS MANY VINTAGE BOUTIQUES, RECORD SHOPS, ART MARKETS, AND FUNKY CAFÉS AND BARS.

Check Me Out:

Flamingo

GROWN UP TABATHA

RAGLA MAGLA

Rose VINTAGE

B BIG TIME

DESERT SNOW

STICKOUT

Top of the Hill

bona

LITTLE TRIP

TO HEAVEN

素今歩 ミカソ SUKONBU MIKAN

FITTING ROOM

4 at a time

THIS IS WHERE I SPENT A LOT OF MY TIME. THERE ARE TOO MANY THRIFTY GEMS!

Open

Sale

FLIPPER'S
good time pancake

I FINALLY TRIED THE LEGENDARY JAPANESE FLUFFY PANCAKES! IT WAS LIKE EATING A CLOUD . . . A TRULY TRANSCENDENT EXPERIENCE.

JUST WALKING AROUND THIS NEIGHBORHOOD PUTS ME IN A GOOD MOOD! I ALSO HAVE A NOSTALGIC FONDNESS FOR SHIMOKITAZAWA BECAUSE I STAYED HERE DURING MY FIRST VISIT TO JAPAN IN 2017.

BIDETS ARE THE FUTURE

I'VE NEVER SEEN A SIT-DOWN TOILET IN JAPAN WITHOUT A BIDET, EVEN IN PUBLIC. IT FELT STRANGE AT FIRST, BUT NOW THAT I'M USED TO USING BIDETS, I WILL NEVER LOOK BACK. YOU'LL EXPERIENCE THE CLEANEST BUM OF YOUR LIFE.

THE JAPANESE LOVE THEIR BIDETS SO MUCH, THERE ARE SEEMINGLY ENDLESS BUTTONS TO CUSTOMIZE YOUR EXPERIENCE. HERE'S A QUICK KEY:

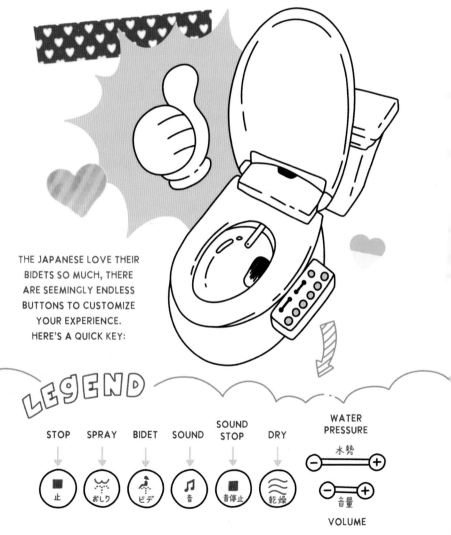

LEGEND

STOP	SPRAY	BIDET	SOUND	SOUND STOP	DRY
止	おしり	ビデ	音	音停止	乾燥

WATER PRESSURE
水勢
⊖ —— ⊕

VOLUME
音量
⊖ —— ⊕

Linguistic CONFUSION

JAPANESE SPEAKERS LOVE USING FOREIGN WORDS, OFTEN IN VERY QUESTIONABLE WAYS. HERE ARE SOME FUNNY SIGNS I ENCOUNTERED!

les mille feuilles
LIBERTÉ

TRANSLATION: **THE CREPE CAKE OF FREEDOM**
FOR SOME REASON, JAPAN IS OBSESSED WITH FRANCE. THIS IS A FLOWER SHOP.

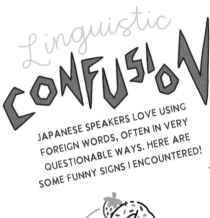

ストロベリー
SUTOBERĪ
ドーナツ
DŌNATSU

TRANSLATION: **STRAWBERRY DONUT**
KATAKANA SCRIPT IS USED TO INTEGRATE FOREIGN WORDS INTO JAPANESE, SOMETIMES TO AN ALMOST ABSURD. I DON'T UNDERSTAND WHY ENGLISH IS USED IN TIMES WHEN THERE IS ALREADY A JAPANESE EQUIVALENT?

greatness COUNTER
SMASH IS THE WAY THAT YOU DEAL WITH LIFE

DWARF BRAVERY

TRANSLATION: **???**
JAPANGLISH REALLY IS A MARVEL UNTO ITSELF.

FACIAL CONFUSION

EVERYONE WEARS MASKS!

REASONS TO WEAR A MASK:

1. SICKNESS
2. ALLERGIES
3. FACE WARMER
4. NO MAKE-UP DAY
5. MEMBER OF A **BŌSŌZOKU** (A SICK BIKE GANG)

Japanese Slang

A MODEST SAMPLING OF JAPANESE PHRASES TO MAKE YOU SOUND MORE LOCAL!

YABAI: "YABAI" LITERALLY MEANS "DANGEROUS," BUT IT'S USED SIMILARLY TO THE WAY "SICK" IS USED IN ENGLISH. IT CAN EXPRESS SENTIMENTS RANGING FROM "TERRIBLE" AND "CRAZY" TO "SURPRISE," "AWE," AND "JOY."

URUSAI: AN EXCLAMATION TO EXPRESS ANNOYANCE OR TO TELL SOMEONE TO SHUT UP.

USO: NO WAY! YOU'RE LYING!

MAJI: SERIOUSLY? FOR REAL?

SAIKOU: THE BEST!

KIMOI: EW, THAT'S GROSS!

UKERU: HAHA, THAT'S FUNNY!

SORE NA: EXACTLY! (AS IN, AN EXCLAMATION OF AGREEMENT.)

BONUS: INTERNET SLANG

W: THIS IS AN EQUIVALENT OF LOL. WHY? BECAUSE THE JAPANESE WORD FOR LAUGH IS 笑い ("WARAI"), SO "W" ACTS AS A SHORTHAND.

JISSHITSU MURYŌ: THIS MEANS "IT'S BASICALLY FREE." YOU CAN SAY THIS WHEN YOU BOUGHT SOMETHING THAT FEELS MUCH MORE VALUABLE TO YOU THAN ITS COST, SO IT ALMOST FEELS FREE.

555: A COMMON ONLINE GAMING EXCLAMATION, "555" MEANS "GO, GO, GO!" ご (GO) IS THE NUMBER 5 IN JAPANESE, SO THIS IS BASICALLY A LITTLE PUN.

MURI: THIS LITERALLY MEANS "I CAN'T," AND IS SAID IN MUCH THE SAME WAY THAT ENGLISH-SPEAKING FANS SAY THE PHRASE WHEN THEIR FAVORITE CELEBRITY OR FICTIONAL SHIP IS CAUSING THEM EMOTIONAL DISTRESS.

EATING LOCAL

TOKYO HAS MORE MICHELIN-STARRED RESTAURANTS THAN ANY CITY IN THE WORLD, SO IT'S NO SURPRISE THAT THERE ARE ENDLESS OPTIONS FOR DELICIOUS DINING. TO MAXIMIZE YOUR FOODIE ADVENTURES, HERE ARE SOME TRIED-AND-TRUE JAPANESE DINING TIPS!

CHEF'S CHOICE: WHEN IN DOUBT, ASK THE CHEF FOR RECOMMENDATIONS BY SAYING:

"OSUSUME WA NAN DESU KA?"

LINING UP: JOIN ANY LONG QUEUES YOU SEE FOR EATERIES. THE FOOD WILL PROBABLY BE AMAZING.

SUSHI: IT'S ACCEPTABLE TO EAT SUSHI WITH YOUR HANDS. WHEN DIPPING NIGIRI SUSHI IN SOY SAUCE, ONLY SATURATE THE FISH SIDE WITH SEASONING.

SIP AND SLURP AWAY: SLURPING IS CONSIDERED A COMPLIMENT TO THE CHEF, SO DON'T HOLD BACK ON THAT RAMEN OR UDON!

SHLURP

MEAL BOOKENDS: IT IS CUSTOMARY TO SAY:

"ITADAKIMASU" AT THE START OF A MEAL AND

"GOCHISOU SAMA DESHITA" AT THE END OF A MEAL.

THESE POLITE PHRASES SHOW APPRECIATION FOR THE FOOD IN FRONT OF YOU, AND ROUGHLY TRANSLATE TO "BON APPÉTIT" AND "THANK YOU FOR THE MEAL."

PAYING: TO ASK FOR THE BILL, SAY THE PHRASE:

"OKANJOU ONEGASHIMASU."

AVOID SAYING "BILL" AS IT SOUNDS SIMILAR TO "BEER" IN JAPANESE, SO YOU MAY BE MIS-INTERPRETED.

寿司

2,143円

RAMEN TICKET: ORDERING AT A RAMEN RESTAURANT IS COMMONLY DONE BY PURCHASING FOOD TICKETS FROM THE VENDING MACHINE RIGHT OUTSIDE THE ESTABLISHMENT. AFTER BUYING THE DISH TICKET(S), HAND THE TICKET(S) TO THE CHEF AT THE COUNTER TO START YOUR ORDER.

ラーメン

CURRY HOUSE CoCo壱番屋

Good smell, Good curry. CoCoICHIBANYA

COCO CURRY IS A JAPANESE FAST CASUAL CHAIN RESTAURANT. BOXED CURRY IS ALREADY TASTY, BUT COCO CURRY IS TRULY NEXT-LEVEL DELECTABLE. THERE ARE DOZENS OF PREMADE OPTIONS, BUT AS THE CURRY HERE IS COMPLETELY CUSTOMIZABLE, IT WOULD BE A SHAME NOT TO TAKE ADVANTAGE OF HAVING ONE TAILORED TO YOUR OWN TASTES. AND UNLIKE MOST "SPICY" JAPANESE FOODS, COCO CURRY DISHES WILL BE SPICY WHEN THEY SAY SPICY. I WOULD NOT GO ABOVE A LEVEL 4 FOR THE FAINT OF HEART— A LEVEL 10 COULD EASILY INDUCE UNPLEASANT BODILY REACTIONS!

WINNIE'S COMBO

CURRY FLAVOR: BEEF
RICE: 200G
SPICE LEVEL: 4-6
EXTRA TOPPINGS: PORK KATSU, EGGPLANT, CORN, SPINACH, MUSHROOM, AND CHEESE

MENU GUIDE

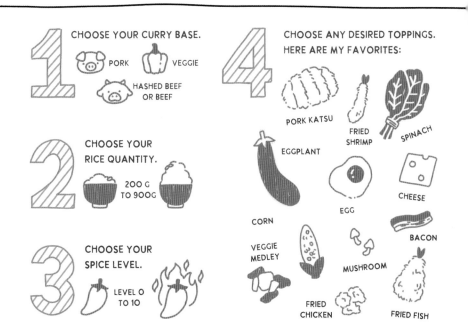

1 CHOOSE YOUR CURRY BASE.

PORK

VEGGIE

HASHED BEEF OR BEEF

2 CHOOSE YOUR RICE QUANTITY.

200 G TO 900G

3 CHOOSE YOUR SPICE LEVEL.

LEVEL 0 TO 10

4 CHOOSE ANY DESIRED TOPPINGS. HERE ARE MY FAVORITES:

PORK KATSU

FRIED SHRIMP

SPINACH

EGGPLANT

EGG

CHEESE

CORN

VEGGIE MEDLEY

MUSHROOM

BACON

FRIED CHICKEN

FRIED FISH

Sangenjaya

cat FEVER

ANOTHER SLEEPY LITTLE NEIGHBORHOOD, OFTEN MENTIONED IN THE SAME BREATH AS KICHIJŌJI, THIS AREA'S MOST PRECIOUS FEATURES ARE THE VINTAGE TRAMLINE (OF WHICH THERE ARE ONLY TWO LEFT IN TOKYO) AND AN OBSESSION WITH CATS.

I'LL TAKE YOU ON A CHARMING RIDE THAT'S PERFECT FOR VIEWING SOME PICTURESQUE SCENERY IN OFTEN BUSTLING TOKYO!

CAN YOU TELL THAT WE REALLY, REALLY LIKE CATS AROUND HERE?

OKASHI

I PASSED BY A DELIGHTFUL AND NOSTALGIC "OKASHI" (SWEETS SHOP) THAT TRANSPORTED ME TO THE '80S! THE NICE OLD LADY GAVE ME SOME EXTRA CANDY.

feline temple

GOTOKU-JI IS A BUDDHIST TEMPLE FILLED TO THE BRIM WITH "MANEKI NEKO," JAPANESE STATUES OF A LUCKY CAT. LEGEND HAS IT THAT A TRAVELING SAMURAI LORD REBUILT THIS TEMPLE TO HONOR A FELINE THAT SAVED HIM FROM AN ONCOMING THUNDERSTORM.

60

shin-ōkubo

TOKYO'S KOREATOWN BOASTS MANY OF THE SAME INSTITUTIONS I LOVED FROM THE KOREATOWN BACK HOME: GOOD FOOD, SPECIALTY GROCERY STORES, POP-CULTURE STORES, AND A QUICK ESCAPE FROM WHAT I'M USED TO.

ahjumma

I TRIED MY FIRST KOREAN HOT DOG! THE ELDERLY WOMAN BEHIND THE COUNTER WAS SO FRIENDLY.

Happy BIRTHDAY

JI-EUN

MIU

WINNIE (ME)

MY FRIENDS JI-EUN AND MIU HAVE CLOSE BIRTHDAYS IN DECEMBER, SO JI-EUN INVITED MIU AND I TO FEAST ON KOREAN BBQ WITH HER TO CELEBRATE. I'M VERY GRATEFUL AS I PROBABLY WOULDN'T HAVE VENTURED TO THIS AREA WERE IT NOT FOR HER!

new year's Traditions

I DIDN'T EXPERIENCE JAPAN'S NEW YEAR'S CUSTOMS FIRSTHAND BECAUSE I LEFT THE COUNTRY BEFORE JANUARY. IT WAS SUCH A SHAME AS THERE ARE SO MANY INTERESTING TRADITIONS FOR THIS HOLIDAY—HOPEFULLY I CAN WITNESS THEM IN THE FUTURE.

FOR MANY JAPANESE, THE NEW YEAR IS SYNONYMOUS WITH "HATSUMŌDE," THE FIRST SHRINE VISIT OF THE YEAR. PEOPLE WAIT PATIENTLY IN LONG QUEUES TO BEGIN THEIR NEW YEAR WITH GOOD FORTUNE.

OSECHI ARE TRADITIONAL JAPANESE NEW YEAR FOODS. THEY ARE PRESENTED IN "JUBAKO," BEAUTIFUL TIERED BOXES SPECIFICALLY MADE TO HOLD AND PRESENT FOOD.

FOR A SHOPAHOLIC LIKE ME, ONE OF THE NEW YEAR'S MOST EXCITING EVENTS IS THE "FUKUBUKURO," A CUSTOM IN WHICH "LUCKY" BAGS FILLED WITH UNKNOWN RANDOM CONTENTS ARE SOLD FOR A SUBSTANTIAL DISCOUNT.

Dear Diary

DECEMBER 23

WHEN I WAS BOARDING MY FLIGHT BACK HOME, IT FELT SURREAL HOW QUICKLY FOUR MONTHS HAD PASSED. IS IT POSSIBLE FOR SOMETHING TO BE EVERYTHING YOU DREAMED OF AND MORE, YET ALSO EXCRUCIATING? I ADMIRED JAPAN DEEPLY FROM AFAR AND WITH LITTLE KNOWLEDGE FOR SO LONG. MY TIME HERE SHOWED ME THAT IT WAS EVERY BIT AS BEAUTIFUL AND WONDERFUL AS I HAD HOPED IT TO BE. I FULFILLED ONE OF MY LIFELONG DREAMS, CONNECTED WITH AMAZING PEOPLE (EVEN ACROSS OUR CULTURAL DIFFERENCES), AND GREW SO MUCH AS A PERSON. AT THE SAME TIME, IT WAS EMOTIONALLY CHALLENGING TO CONSTANTLY BE FACED WITH ISOLATION FROM MY LOVED ONES, A LANGUAGE BARRIER, AND A LOSS OF CONTROL. STILL, I WOULDN'T TRADE THE UPS AND DOWNS FOR ANYTHING. IT WAS A TRANSFORMATIVE EXPERIENCE THAT I WILL BE FOREVER GRATEFUL FOR. THIS JOURNEY REVEALED WHAT I TRULY VALUE IN LIFE, AND THAT'S SOMETHING I'LL HAVE WITH ME FOREVER. I CAN'T WAIT TO COME BACK SOMEDAY SOON AND SHOW JAPAN WHAT THE NEW WINNIE IS LIKE!

ACKNOWLEDGMENTS

TO THE LOVE OF MY LIFE, REID: YOU BRING ME LIGHT, LAUGHTER, JOY, AND MORE. YOUR ENCOURAGEMENT MEANS THE WORLD TO ME. I'M SO LUCKY FOR GETTING TO SPEND MY LIFE WITH YOU. I LOVE YOU! TO MY KITTIES, MOMO AND CALCIFER: YOU MAKE ME SMILE EVERYDAY, EVEN WHEN YOUR POOPS ARE MEGA STINKY . TO MY FRIENDS: YOU ARE MY FOUND FAMILY AND I LOVE YOU ALL. THANK YOU ESPECIALLY TO THE ONES WHO HAD A FIRST LOOK AT THIS BOOK: ANNA, YUNI, JOOYOUNG, ABBY, AND ASHNA! JUHO, THANK YOU FOR THE BUBBLE TEA THAT HELPED ME TO THE FINISH LINE, AND ASHER, THANK YOU FOR ENDURING COLORING HELL WITH ME. TO MY MUSABI FAMILY: THANK YOU MIU, JI-EUN, MIOTO, RIHO TEDDY SENSEI, AND JULIA SENSEI FOR MAKING MY TRIP UNFORGETTABLE. TO THE ULYSSES PRESS TEAM: THANK YOU FOR HELPING ME TURN MY PASSION PROJECT INTO A REALITY. A SPECIAL SHOUT-OUT TO CASIE AND SHELONA FOR THE INITIAL SUPPORT, CLAIRE FOR BEING THE BEST BOSS, RENEE FOR THE INDISPENSABLE KNOWLEDGE, BRIDGET FOR REMINDING ME TO CHILL, AND YESENIA FOR BEING MY ROCK.

ABOUT THE AUTHOR

WINNIE LIU IS A CHINESE-AMERICAN ILLUSTRATOR AND DESIGNER WITH A PASSION FOR ALL THAT IS PINK. SHE LOVES WHIMSICAL STORYTELLING AND CREATING CUTE THINGS FOR THE YOUNG AND YOUNG AT HEART. WHEN SHE ISN'T DESIGNING BOOKS AT ULYSSES PRESS, SHE IS THE FREELANCE ARTIST KNOWN AS "WINNIE IS PINK." IN HER FREE TIME, SHE CAN BE FOUND SCOUTING GOOD FOOD (ESPECIALLY IF IT'S SPICY), EXPLORING THE CITY FOR ARTISTIC INSPIRATION, AND TABLING AT ARTIST ALLEYS SELLING HER STATIONERY AND ACCESSORIES. WINNIE LIVES IN BROOKLYN, NEW YORK, WITH HER PARTNER AND TWO ADORABLE CATS. FIND HER PORTFOLIO AND SHOP AT WWW.WINNIEISPINK.COM AND CONNECT WITH HER ON SOCIAL MEDIA @WINNIEISPINK.